Amused

By G.M. Karam,
muse and bemused

Muse: the goddess or the power regarded as inspiring a poet, artist, thinker, or the like.

Amused

Copyright © 2024 by G.M. Karam

Front cover, inner photos, and eyes credited to Allyssa Milan, Model-Artist

Front Cover, Part 1 photos by Tashi Negron
Part 2 photo by Ally Boobior
Back cover photo by the author

with four photo-digital artworks
by Illustrator Ashley Peterkin-Blackwood

Publisher
Poetic Design Services
(poeticdesignservices@gmail.com)

First Edition
ISBN: 979-8-218-36577-6 Paperback

Printed in the United States of America

For further information or to contact the Author, please email
poeticdesignservices@gmail.com

Introduction

Muses.

This collection of poems honors the muse, exploring the unseen and profound role they play in the lives of people, from all walks of life.

"the goddess or the power regarded as inspiring a poet, artist, thinker, or the like."[1]

I play a muse. But more often, I am influenced by them. I began to write poetry and occasionally prose because of the passions and thoughts instilled in me by muses. In the last five years, as part of my own personal Renaissance, I have inspired and been inspired, but on the whole, the impact of the muse on my life has been profound.

Poetry, for me, represents moments in time that define a feeling, an emotion, a reflection, or an inflection point of being, that is so powerful that it must be captured for my remembrance, or conveyed to others.

My muses happen to be all women, probably because they most strongly arouse my romantic passions. Some have been long, deep relationships, and others had more transitory, nevertheless, each having a critical impact.

The encouragement afforded by a muse is subtle. Their presence, the world view they model, their own beliefs and vision, give one

---

[1] Dictionary.com

the permission to see things in themselves. They don't gift you talent, or joy, or creativity, or any of the outcomes of their proximity. Those things are present, but sometimes buried by regret, anxiety, confidence, and the emotional baggage of life. Their counsel or insight or simply their energy, unlocks the doors to one's own capabilities.

I had permission to be myself. I was supported in being who I was as a man, as a human, as a lover, as a person floating in society touching the spirits of others.

It all starts with me.

Many of these poems find their source in a particular woman, though sometimes they are amalgams of sparks. Yet two women have played life changing roles with their awakening of my spirit. They have spawned many written works, because of the revelations they awoke.

The first, pulled me from an emotional burning car, only to remind me who I was. At the time, that was the change I needed. The second, upended my view of myself, or rather, burnished my belief that I could be this different and superior version of a man.

A variety of others have colored in the many dimensions of me that bring me to the place I am, and prepare me for new journeys. At least one is a woman I never met - I never knew her real name - yet we were in each other's pockets for almost 18 months.

Largely this is a body of work centering on romance, love, eroticism, and erotic experiences; all reflections of who I am and how I feel about human interaction. They are mine: creative outcomes of my spirit and the women who have carried influence with it, but they are also human. May you see yourself and your path at least partially illuminated in mine.

And if not, then enjoy the amusement park of my life. Like any visit to the carnival, half the fun is watching others.

The first part of the book reflects more romantic explorations, like riding a gentle Ferris Wheel. The second book shares erotic adventures – akin to a Roller Coaster.

Even if you don't get on the rides, you can imagine the feelings and thrills!

GK

January 2024

Acknowledgements

I am deeply indebted to the many readers of working copies of the poems. Kendra Hillier volunteered her editorial eye for the introduction, and Allyssa Milan provided insights on the content and overall design as well as her personal contributions to its visual elements.

The muses shall go unattributed. Some know who they are, and others may see their influence or perhaps never see the book in print. Nonetheless without their inspiration, this would not exist. I am filled with gratitude.

Part A: Ferris Wheel

Dewy Leaf

muse

Breakfast on Friday

Celestial

The Gift

One

Coconut

Soul's Food

Currents

Clarity

Poetry of the Soul

Flying Faster

Tick Tock

Visit

Presence

Glory

Dinner For Two

Dewy Leaf

Early morning on a Caribbean beach

Eden is shamed by the tranquility and rare
beauty.

I seat myself on the wooden chair
letting my toes slither
in the cool sand.

Caressing my arm was a
giant leaf of iridescent green.

Atop were scores of petite drops of dew —
fresh from the labors of
the nighttime air.

They caught my attention as the
casual ocean breeze bounced
them into each other like
couples joining up and
weaving across
a dance floor.

**The salty air stroked my cheeks and
persuaded my eyes to lull.**

———————————— // ————————————

I feel the sensual music fill my ears,
your face next to mine,
your slender waist nestled into my arm,
my hand linked with yours.

Unable to resist the motion of your hips
shifting to the hypnotic
rhythm of the music,

**my lips seek your ear whispering...
You light a fever on my soul.**

I feel your smile as your lips reciprocate
with familiar nibbles about my ear.

Like the wind against the frond,
the dew drops re-arrange
and the dance floor
and music along with them.

**In a shimmering moment our partners
change.**

**To the heat of Salsa Cubano
gyrates a tall man
with piercing dark eyes,
olive skin and full lips.**

**His lanky build is wrapped by
a silken dark suit with a
shocking bright white shirt.**

Caught in my gaze, was you
moving with erotic abandon
in syncopated beat with
this captivating partner.

In a glance, you toss your grin
and devil's eyes in my direction
to acknowledge a woman of equal
appearance who has materialized on my arms.

**With jet black hair,
matching wide eyes, pale complexion,
she bobs and slinks in her form-fitting
satin dress portraying her cleavage,
supple legs, and muscled body.**

Both of our couples cross the dance floor by
instinct and blind passion.

The intensifying music drives the blood heat
ever spiraling out of control.

In a moment of crescendo we accept our fates
and relinquish ourselves
to the ocean of desire.

Two kisses,
with the blessing and
witness of Satan himself,
compete on either
end of the dance floor.

**Open lips, darting flesh, and the coming
together of two pairs of bodies screaming
out pure frenzy.**

———————————— // ————————————

The ocean.
The breeze.
And once again the drops of dew blur.
The dance floor is gone.

I sense your aura –
fingers sliding down my arm
in the simplest affection.

In a timeless moment,
you seated in the wooden chair aside me,
on the quiet beach,
in the early morn.

Your ever-present smile and radiant eyes
draw my attention.

Rising from the seat,
you climb elegantly across my lap.

Your seventy-five years have not
dwindled your agility in the least.

Cautious movements that still
bear the fluid swing of your Latin birth.

Of what were you daydreaming?
   You ask, your hands holding my face.

Just the dewy leaf,
   I reply, with a smile towards
      my green companion.

You were swaying. Was there more?
                  Oh, we danced on the leaf.

   With a laugh you bite the tip of my nose.
      And slip into my arms
      as dawn light melts the dew.

muse

"the goddess or the power regarded as inspiring a poet, artist, thinker, or the like."

i long to create
art, beauty are painted by culinary works

yet the artist gets t r a p p e d
in the lane of talent

my muse tickled the iMaGiNaTiOn
think different, be excited again

       never asking or demanding,
       the muse sways, invigorates

i felt novice, and my muse eyed silently.
did she care? is there deliberation?
or is it pixie dust falling off her wand?

motivations were unimportant
she just is a connected soul,
peeking into my own spirit.
was she curious?

am I unique in her experience?
or just another who feels her thrill?

one cannot be a muse,
one can become – only in another's eyes

when she and I one day join, i wonder, what
will i become?

Breakfast on Friday

Food.
Shelter.
Water.
Love.

The four elements of human need.

Breakfast, I come to your home for breakfast.

A cherished repast, for it is taken at a
treasured point in the day, it's dawn.

I arrive to the aromas of your preparation.

Intoxicating
coffee.

Freshly cooked
eggs.

Crispy pumpernickel
toast.

I greet you with an embrace,
        and you devour me with affection
                as if I am your first meal.

Holding our passions at bay,
    we take our posts around your table,
        close but enough separation to eat,
            lest we become the main course.

An effortless conversation
        is occasionally seasoned with
                kisses and caresses.

Eggs, served ever so easily,
        are consumed with hearty fervor,
                accompanied by Allah's gift
                to the garden,
                        the sweetest saffron
                mangoes.

                                        Food.
                                     Shelter.
                                       Water.

Woven into every moment lives a love.

                                        Eyes,
                                      smiles,
                                      laughs,
                                        hugs,
                                  and kisses.

Breakfast ended.

Simple.

                                        Food.
                                     Shelter.
                                       Water.

                  And love.

Celestial

Many faces,
　　　　　colors,
　　　　　　　　　　expression

Who is the woman:
　　　　　　　　none? all?

From a distance, there is only a lens

　　　Behind the camera, gentle humanity

　　　Obscured by image, stage, seduction

　　　Her spirit a guarded poker hand

　　　　　Yet occasionally revealed,

　　　　　　　by respect,

　　　　　　　affection

One card,

　　　　　　　　two cards

Creative flashes,

arc behind a luxurious gaze

　　　A polished wit, shares kind warmth

　　A heart that speaks with honest delicacy

—————————//—————————

An astral glow to your image

A man's hand, senses your refined profile

Your bloom entrancing his emotions

The focus of

your easy smile

warms

Your presence

S T I L L S

the room

He stops,

words pause,

gripped tenderly

This moment

A W A I T S

one day

The Gift

We give gifts. To one another. To others.
We give. We receive. Fully, or not. But we do.

A journey of personal thought, growth.
A marriage of intention and consent.

I give a thing, an object.
                    You receive in affection.

You give your spirit.
                    I embrace with thirst.

I gave my hands, to nourish, a balm.
                    You drink their power and
                        ease in your body.

I give your face a field of its own.
                    You take the space to cleanse
                        and search your voice.

You give an experience.
                    I dwell in paradise.

I give an experience.
                    Your spirit, treasured.

Humanity intertwined, gifts move effortless

    Floating on river of affection, respect.
                Always.

            Renewed. And cherished.
                Always.

One

A million kisses

Your soft lips taste me

Your impassioned tongue darts

My mouth melting to yours

My skin afire

My heart churns

My blood steams

Desire
      i
  B   l l
        O
      W s
         from my spirit

One kiss. One **thousand**. One MILLION.

One.

Coconut

Anticipated, still unexpected

Your emotions   S   p   d into me
              E
        e   E

A spiritual *mist* entered my soul
        at every p • int

                I was desired,
                  compelled,
                    needed,
                      loved

You surfaced each passion
        by presence
        a l o n e

  My homage to you, the energy of my being

Given through
hands,
fingers,
tips,
touch

  A tropical experience R(eveale)D itself

  A luxurious scent, as I honored your form

  Care, affection and inescapably lust

    We left a journey in our wake
    And an everlasting reminder

Soul's Found

The ether of the world is smoked in mystic

Yet people a life apart,
                as different can be, unite

I cannot fathom the warmth we found

I cannot imagine the fluid intimacy

I cannot conceive of a time without you

I need the honesty of your embrace
   I need the affection of your grin
      <u>I need the passion of your want</u>

I long for the vigor of your laughter
   I long for the calm of your thoughts
      <u>I long for the tenderness of your hands</u>

From that first burning kiss,
                to every moment since...

I live in awe of the **magic** that brought

                        two souls together

I love for respect of the souls we share

And the grandeur of a **mysterious** force

Today is a point of discovery,
                endless in either direction

Perpetually, endless

Currents

Darts of red illuminated the morning sky
Early birds form a symphonic landscape

Seated, the warm mist arising from coffee,
we blend into the unraveling day

Silently,
we drink the happiness of the moment
reluctant to disturb the brief artistry
in an endless arc of spiritual life

The heat from a rising sun, coats my skin,
an invitation to join

The crystalline lake,
met the sand like a knife edge

On closer look,
tiny lives hid beneath the watery glass,
like a mirage

We walked,
our toes disturbing
the placid world of the shoreline,
like giant waterfowl

At least you walked with grace,
the female soul always did.
I lumbered,
doing a poor imitation of art,
but I made you smile

"I could be dead tomorrow you know",
as I chose words fitting of my gait

**"Why would you spoil this soulful beauty
with such a morbid conversation"**

*"It's not morbid, it's a fact.
The doctor will put me to sleep,
and I may not come back"*

"Of course you will, don't dwell on this"

*"I'm not.
I just think of it,
one day here in this happiness,
and tomorrow, nothing"*

"You are ruining my happiness"

*"I am just one,
of the trillions of currents of existence.
Not happy. Not sad. Just here"*

"I like your current so I will be unhappy"

*"Maybe.
And if my grandfather,
had been allowed to board the Titanic,
then we would not be in this place"*

**"But that didn't happen and I don't want to
think of you gone"**

*"I think I'll come back as a cat.
One minute me, go to sleep,
and then I'm a cat"*

"How do you know you will come back at all?"

"So that you don't miss me"

In a moment you burst with laughter
And the impact of your fist on my shoulder,
a reminder of your spirited personality

The light filled the world with joy
My arc of life flowed in the grace of now
With yours

Clarity

Feminine power.

       HAS NO EQUAL.

Pain.
      Struggle.
            Desire.
                  Purpose.

      A primordial soup for women.

Stirred and encouraged and curated.

Then the birth of child, clarity.

Then stand back.
        Sit up.
           Eyes wide open.

Men, she will...

      Challenge. Need. Share.

In open heart, she will invigorate.

      Pray for this woman.

      She is what we seek.

Poetry of the Soul

There is a poetry in your soul,
as it explores who you are,
your now,
your presence
                    in the world of people.

Your poetry
        has tremendous emotion and passion,
        wrapped in rhythms and wisdom.

                        Poetry needs freedom.
                    From freedom comes idea,
            from idea comes joy and creation,
                and from those the world
                grows in new experience.

Your soul
        writes

            words and
            phrases and
            couplets, and sonnets.

People feel them in all their forms,
your image,
        conversations,

            art,

            motion.
All of your expressive forms.

And those who open themselves
to receive the wholeness
of your spirit,
        are forever touched and transformed.

With such an

 e x p a n s i v e
soul,

you ask of those around you to grow
and dance with you.

To   s t r e t c h   themselves
to wrap their own feelings
around yours in thoughtful embrace.

I do so,
     unreservedly and
          with anticipation
               of each new moment.

Where will your
poetic soul
take us next ?

Flying Faster

On the high perch, pressed by the constant
weight of the breeze is the roost to the
handsome falcon couple.

She watches with full sharp eyes.
Crimson highlights in her feathers,
glow in the rays of light descending.

Her talons, sharp, deadly, smooth held onto
their footing.

> She ponders her mate next to her,
> wondering what their action might be.
> **Rest? Plan? Conquer? Feed?**

She glances around her world.
Nothing escaped her watch.
Attentive to movement, prey or aggressor.

Her mate.
The sky.
The horizon.
The ground.
Over and over.

> He sits close to her.
> His jet black body gleams as
> if his coat were lacquered.
> His full size hovers over her, as though
> his physical presence were protection.

> His forceful claws grip intently,
> yet gently nudging hers.
> Circumstance?
> Or affection?
> Do these fearsome raptors love?
> Do they touch beyond instinct?
> Do they crave belonging, simple contact?

He sweeps the earth with rhythm.
His eyes study terrain,
shifting in a staccato tempo.
He swivels to his mate.
She senses his stare and turns to him.

Their vision in lock, thoughts
flow quickly amid the two avian lovers.

In unison and elegance,
they spread their wings and lift.

It is time to hunt.

The pair glide into the air, broad powerful
wings outstretched to coax the sky to keep
them aloft.

They move swiftly as their strategy shows.
A thousand times in practiced execution,
she begins to move forward.

She is smaller, lighter,
but accelerates beyond her size,
flying faster and
ahead of her man.

He separates while his aggressive partner
slices through the air with ever increasing
velocity.

The prey senses the looming terror and starts
to dash across the meadow with abject horror
weighing on its mind.

She stares at dinner, unrelenting focus.

The beast has broken away from its peers
in a clumsy act of self-preservation.
Sometimes they see her coming.
It makes no difference in the end.

With speed and grace, she has descended from
heaven to earth. Finesse spreads her wings to
slow as she approaches.

The prey shifts and weaves as fear burns in
its soul and fires its survival.
No matter.

In an explosion of ferocity, sleek
blackness appears out of the setting sun,
like an evil apparition.

**In a blur, the quarry becomes imprisoned by
merciless claws.**

She joins her mate, to revel in the kill.

Again, they have together delivered a bounty.

Once in motion,
it was the rare prey that could evade their
partnership.

The mates glance at each other as
the big male sits above their winnings.

Stern eyes, loathsome to those around,
speak differently to each other.

Come, we have seen triumph again.
Now we enjoy the efforts.

With a casual twist of his beak,
the big falcon, tears the throat from
the mammal in his tight grasp.

He delivers his gruesome killing blow with no
more thought than stretching his wings in
the morning sun.

In defiance of nature itself,
he steps back.
She moves forward.

With the art of a gifted carnivore,
she prepares the treasure.

They share the meal in determined flurry.

Unusual.. but maybe, she was the better chef,
and they both knew it.

**Perhaps on occasion,
people should love as falcons do.**

Tick Tock

The hours pass with *l o n g i n g*

Or **A g o N Y.**

When do you return?

Swiss time, Italian time. Any time.

You dance in my heart.

You smile in my spirit.

You fuel the fires of passion.

The **clock.**

The hours.

When do I have you again?

Visit

My body
D
E
S
C
E
N
D
E
D
s l o w l y onto the bed

Twelve hours before,
you had lain,
each contour of your feminine
arranged like

Renaissance art

I observed then.
Taken by the perfection of the moment.
It's sits in my head, cast like a sculpture
destined for perpetuity

The image stays with me,
but sown into it,
are the moments and sentiments of

today,
yesterday,
our history,
deep into souls past

Conversations, touches, emotions, tensions
are the clay of this human sculpture.

I am older, and with wisdom comes an
efficiency of dissecting each relationship.
<u>But not this one.</u>

Without any model of experience,
we both tread virgin land,
marveling in discovery but
also mystified by unknowns.

———————————//———————————

i rest on white sheets.
only you and i share presence here.

Your cellular electricity leaves residue.
A slight heat of you, us, life.

My spirit mines your energy so I feel you

I sense all the appearances of
your expressions.

Every smile.
Every sadness.
Every passion.
Every calm.
Each pensive moment.
And the quiet of your sleep.

That was last night.
It is morning now. I have been up.
Feeling an easy late summer breeze.
Maybe I will go back and lie down
just to draw you again.

———————————//———————————

i cleaned up the kitchen. it felt wrong.
as though i was wiping the memories away.

The cutting board strewn with bits of cheese
that you crave at any hour.

Plates from dining miracles I made for us.
They feel magical because you see them so.

The empty glasses are testaments to the
laughter and knowledge and purest life,
recorded by their use.

Wrapping paper from endless surprises that I
concocted for my infatuation with the child's
joy you share in receiving.

I wish everyone in the world could feel the
glee of a reveal the way you do.

Humanity would be so much happier.

I wish I did. I'm just not very good at it.

———————— // ————————

I introduced you to my baby birds.
I had been hoping beyond hope
they would still be here.

I have lived with nature's avian touch for a
month and begged them to remain
until you could share what I feel.

The exhilaration of that introduction.
Baby birds, meet my love.
My love, meet the baby birds.

Your bond with the energy of
life and world
fostered a deeper sensation in me.

And now witness to your light feeds mine.

They wondered where you were today.

———————— // ————————

The car got a workout.
  I like driving with you.
    The dialog alone, but it's more.

The roads are familiar now.
    Witnesses to the frequent occasions
      together in a 50 mile radius.

Bridges,
        tunnels,
              bodegas,
                    cats.

I know how to pack for road trips now.
                            For you.

It's been a couple of weeks.
                Where will we go next?

———————— // ————————

i wonder if your presence intimidates the
other women in my life.

            My heart is open.
          I won't hide anymore.
      It took four decades to find myself.
          And that's a celebration.

              Here you are.
                Front.
                Center.

          Yes I have someone.
    She is not the only presence in my life,
              but she is here.
          She is my Companheira.
          It's a Portuguese word.
                It's perfect.

        She calls me Companheiro.

———————— // ————————

This visit affirmed our mutual existence.

Words,
music,
food,
touch,
affection.

Re-affirmation doesn't sit right as a word.

The journey goes new places every time.

How can you re-affirm something that carves
new history each time?

I am older.
When I am gone, she can re-affirm us.
It will be frozen time then.

Or maybe not.

Presence

the human spirit leaves it's footprints
wherever it travels

as cast concrete, they're permanent to me

i cannot feel the spirits of those
i do not know,
                    but i am aware of them

i sit in a building, two centuries aged,
i sense the history of souls,
and markers left behind

but i can't embrace them
                    yet you i feel

as i sat in the car today,
as empty as it was,
you rushed into my pores

            i sat there endless moments, absorbing

seat position spoke of your shorter body,
            mastering and commanding the travel

i first felt your energy
                    imprinted in my home

rooms, couch, table, shower, bedroom, bed
sheets, pillows

places we travel in New York
hotels, restaurants, theaters
Macy's forever

today is different
profound because i walk in your history,
                    not ours

for years, this new city was your old one

places i journeyed,
　　　you have left your cast countless times

my mind squints, and you appear

　　　　　　　in the aisles,
　　　　　　　in the book stacks,
　　　　　　　on the grass,
　　　　　　　your presence shouts

what I feel about it is mine to choose
　　　you can't possibly control that
　　　　　　　your energy could be years old

i conjure emotions on my own

i can have all colors –
mad, sad, glad, happy, scared
anything in between

　　　i see your smile, i emote warmth from it
　　　　　　　and i am wrapped in happy

it's what i choose

Glory

Both *glory* and **suffering**

Bookends of *ecstasy* and **surrender**

Common emotions, visions, ideas

When we hold, face, and touch,
the bodies churn need,
then fire and water

Distant, our spirits join
oceans of tears
to tides of love

Wide welcome shores of human experience

The bond, *together* or **apart**

Sinewed muscle of the heart

Champions through worry, need, anger

Each breath, calm to ease the hunger

An aura present across the sea

Or found in warmth against our breast

Always our burdens triumphed by us

Eyes hold, lip clasp, fingers kiss

We find our best, in union

Dinner for Two

"Welcome and please be seated. "

Music chatters.

Trumpets, trombones, piano, and drums light
up the room with passion and
echoes of fresh sound.

*"The Mezze is very good tonight.
May I get you drinks?"*

We gaze at each other. Our arrival still a
mystery. The miles apart collapse to
a dinner table.

Together, we explore a destiny we never knew.
In our 50s, to have such emotions,
such need,
returns an innocence of youth,
paired with the wisdom of experience.

Lively conversations.
Petite culinary treats.
Impassioned strains of jazz.

———————————//———————————

*"Your salads will arrive soon,
shall I bring the wine"*

The saxophone begins a teasing exchange
with the piano.
Older but playful.

Complex experienced flavors splash our
plates of greens and colors.

Sixty year-olds revel in life uncovered,
a world opened to our whims.
It is our buffet of adventures.

We marvel at the journey taken,
how we found future,
a path unplanned but fateful.

————————//————————

"Allow me to clear the table,
as dinner is served"

Soothing melodies rise from the trumpet.
Layered with rhythms from guitar,
double bass, and easy percussion.

Sounds rise and fall,
to carry us through the longer,
measured tastes of the ocean
and the land,
of culture and imagination.

As we navigate our seventies,
our bond is woven with fabric,
a wide spectrum of ideas, scents,
and moments of celebrations.

Each step together is the same
but as new as our first.

————————//————————

"I am happy that the food was to your
liking. And now a small dessert perhaps?
And coffee or tea, or some port?"

The band found an easy, soulful place.
The piano owns the sound with calm yet
playful brass accents.

Sweet and salt so delicate, our aged fingers
pluck slowly. Our movements a careful waltz.

After three decades,
    history no longer matters.

We are here, now, the moments.

We came together.

We will leave together.

            I take your hand in mine.

        I lean over slowly to kiss you.

The clock stops. The fire has not.

        "Please come again!"

The music remains.

PART B: Roller Coaster

tonight

The Kiss

The River

the taste of love

Four Days/Three Nights

Satin Rose

Love Song

Bookends

Perfect

Moonbeams

Sunrise Ocean

At Rest

Photograph

Devotion

Forced

Relinquish

tonight

it was a very special night...
this one, i remember.

i look in those eyes and ...

                              like **tonight,**
                    when you were so close,
            i longed to drink every emotion
                that was going into the body

tonight,
i was so full of emotions
i could play every actor in the theatre ...

                         and **tonight,**
               i had you under my hands
                      you were all mine
               and you let go so readily

you let your soul free
and it all came to my hands,
so perfect and at ease

                    tonight,
          i am so aroused still
            but such is life,
          it was only **tonight**

The Kiss

Barriers dropped.   **Passion released.**

Lips, tenderness molded to me.
A dance without music, arms entwine.

Joining. I am drawn. Lust. Love. Intimacy.
Taste. Need. Warmth. Unrestrained.

Bodies melt like swirled wax,
fired by the kiss.

The cauldron of desire boils anew, fed from
the common flame.

Time crawls.   **Today. This day.**
                    I wish you to feel.

No speculation. Just clarity. I want.
Logic cast aside, spirit prevailing.

Can it last forever?
How far can I join with just my lips?

Time pauses.

                    I can't release.

My soul, connected to my body, connected to
your body, connected to your soul.

Electricity flows between us.

And then it stops.   **Today.**

The River

My finger traces the rivers journey,

    s l o w
        a n d
             m e a n d e r i n g

The smooth
surface of your body,
provides the   **landscape**

                The watershed begins
                  with your face
            follows the first turn
              as my touch traces
                your long neck

                The waters eddy
                as I maneuver
              the gentle bend
              to your shoulders

        A slow path   over steady
              inviting wetness,
      begging my whole being to dive in

I turn the rounded corner to

    S
        L
            I
                D
                    down your arm

      Facing me, you smile and giggle
        sensing my whimsical touch,
     yet you know the stirring within

My fingers cross a waterfall and

D
   E
      S
        C
          E
            N
              D
              to your side,
              as the river
              etches a
              contour over
              your ribs,
              your waist,
              and then your
              hips

As my

        fingers move
        with
        painstaking
        patience,

        your lip bitten
        your eyes close

        and
        a
        M O A N

        escapes your throat

Along the

     U   D   L   T   N
     n   u   a   i   g

          landscape of your hips,
        I dutifully trail your thigh,
      the rivers' journey to your toes,
                awaiting

Your
thighs
squeeze
in
a
sweet
agony

The long trek is complete,
            my hand on your foot,
                    your skin seeking
                    more

    Perhaps the journey upstream

        will be taken

            by

            my

kisses

the taste of love

i relish the instruction, *sauté over low heat*

i feel the experience fully in my hands

fingers moving slowly, with deliberate motion

a meandering process, asking patience to move
towards success

it's too early to sample
time and flair required

i am aware how i relish a leisurely pace

if i move gradually maybe time
                    will last l o n g e r

      when you get older the clock can be an
      unwelcome roommate

though, a fast boil can be the right heat
                    energy exploding like a reaction

then returning to the low simmer ...
                    was it an hour?

minutes pass
              a little of this
                    a little of that

the nerve endings in my digits
              indulge in the easy motions

following guidance with care and respect

i imagine how things may taste for you,
              when this treasure reaches perfection

would it be the same for me?

no. uniqueness of the human spirit says no

a small seduction begins with your tongue

my craftwork teases and flirts

your warm lips and mouth allow for more

        but always it is your luscious soul

           where a sunrise is found

emotions, meet senses, stirred in a pot of

           memories
           fantasies
           beliefs
           hopes

     this is destination for any experience,
       taste though is all surrounding

taste: seen, touched, smelled,
               savored, even heard

   but that sixth, declares... *i love it!*

Four Days/Three Nights

Fates give choices,
　　　　　but we must see and decide

Meeting her was an inflection point

Mimicking a weak signal,
　　　　she *s l i d e s* into a conversation

The emotions and spirit sense,
　　　　　　I'll never understand

Each word amplifies,
　　　　　　　it feels … **right**

With increasing momentum,
　　　came the unplanned escape,
　　　　　　to weave new bonds

———————————//———————————

Friday

Heart beating, with mere expectation

Old world plush

Soft musical strains echo from a sleek grand

Who else sat here,
in decades of classic experiences?

A love seat,
a kaleidoscope of colors and pillows,
it spoke **luxury**

I waited.
The curve of emotions accelerated,
with each T-I-C-K of the **CLOCK**

Waiter, oh Waiter..
he appeared,
starched peering across his lens,
brought a libation

The chilled conical glass wrapped itself
about my careful mixture
of Russia and France

Still I sat,
staring at the dance of patrons,
like it's a ship's gangway

Searching for the one

Patience rewarded, my rendezvous E n t e r e d

S l o w,
a silhouette from a 1950s glamour shoot

A stack of curly **chocolate** locks,
topped a perfect figure eight

Her dark warm gleam keep me in sight,
while her smile erupted with kindness,
at the moment of truth

I held her,

could she hear my chest

S C R E A M I N G ?!

Our sojourn begins...

Oh Garçon... food drinks

Where could we begin?

HOW could we tell
so many stories
in a short evening

HOW was it possible
for a two mouths to join,
so **perfectly,**
despite the furtive glances
of others

The world f a d e d to **black**
as just we remained

Lost in ourselves,
our bodies,
our dialog,
our needs

I would never be the same,
nor lack appreciation
of that profound thought

We left late,
for a journey down the city of lights,
unable to dampen the fire

Windows down and bodies aroused,
two teenagers played down the avenue
from one street to another

Today would beget tomorrow,
after all we had a **plan**

It had to ...
my bosom would not bear being with her
but once.

———————— // ————————

Saturday

Noon, the breakfast hour

Coffee? I have just the place

Her eyes widen, glow, awe...
me or the food?

An early walk through Italy
and culinary offerings

She imagines her travels to **Rome,**
but wandering **New York**

I gave her a dream
as we flew to the building top...
sunlight d
r
i
p
p
i
n
g
Italian brunch
She touched,
she kissed,
she loved,
because she does

The day could have played out
unmoved from glory
but,
a new pleasure awaited

———————————//———————————

A rare celebration tomorrow
needs a garment today

She had a new sensual experience
- that's how she savored it

One outfit, another outfit –
    a man with the <u>eye of a woman</u>,
      but the instinct and <u>desire of a man</u>

She would stroll the catwalk …

        Yes ? No ?

        Stunning.

The ladies stared –
                Who was she?
                Who was he?
         And how did he know?

My hands cupped her feet gently,
tending her as lovers should,

        one pair,
        two pair,
    finding the right pair

      As the our day coasted to a close,
        another transition

          In the mirror,
      she performed her ritual art

        Her nude body enticed
    the *s_l_o_w_e_s_t graze* of my hands,
    as if she was a harp to my fingers

        I love these moments,
      the transformation,
    a reveal born of intimacy

   At the close, a **long** ride to her evening,
        fingers intertwined
      and our spirits sewn tighter

———————//———————

Sunday

Unexpected timing

A big day,
she was a glory,
a silvery shining delight

Late night rendezvous at water's edge,
midnight,
the moment calling

A return to home,
to share,
be human,
feel warmth,

took an unexpected fork

Her heartbroken soul poured open

I bore witness to a hurt,
and applied the balm of calming support,
a wisdom of years,
and spiritual energy

Into the wee hours,
the story unfurled,
until it was no more,
and only exhaustion lay ahead

As the Sun rose over the glass towers
I roused to begin another journey

I awoke her gently,
her angelic face a picture of solace,
her voice at ease,
and her mind at peace.

A kiss, and then gone

———————— // ————————

Monday

Our <u>odyssey</u> has been a collection of
serendipitous moments

Some <u>days</u> unfold with designs that
depart from expectation
yet beautiful

An <u>idea</u>, and then,
a return to the beginning,
not turning back the clock,
but deeper study,
instead

In <u>comfort</u> once again,
our starched friend
caring for oral delights

She is exquisite in her look,
manner, affection and verve

Each **kiss** witness by a crowd,
but unseen by us

Laughter, exploration and
unvarnished happiness

And finally a close to the day

A sentimental movie scene,
with the tenderness of black and white film,
I bid her safe journey
as she boarded the train.

à la prochaine
And I waved

Satin Rose

There is an art to a woman's form

Curves,
    limbs,
        radiance,
            that speak soft presence

On my bed, the sheets entwine the image

Gentle fabric transforms nudity
    to *erotic* l a n d s c a pe

Her position,
    askance among the folds of cloth

She smiles warmly as I watch at the door

My companion has become sculpture

The bed, her pedestal

The bedroom, a gallery

I,

the private audience,

blessed

Love Song

Long limbs circle with a musical sway

                              Tightly held, the electricity
                                   of arousal sparks

A pause, eyes connect, a boundary crossed

   A flood a passion erupts, held back no more

Violins play their melody of need

   Eyes give way to lips, to French expressions

The instrument held tight,
plays fervent strains

                               The music wanders,
                              shedding layers,
                                to a raw tempo

Seeking the climactic moment,
the staccato beat slows, uncertain

                            Compositions take time

The musician will return to conclude

                                 Another day

Bookends

It begins with an awkward instant

<I've never done this>

Turn? Kiss? Embrace? Are there rules?

<Did I seem like a fool>

My eyes take a full measure of drink
Edgy, relaxed, and quietly sensual

<She's gorgeous>
<Don't tell me, tell her>

Words stumble from my mouth
Have I regressed to my teens?

Seated, the Japanese sense of propriety
A candle affixed to the table, chaperones
An impediment, but not an obstacle

Velvet palms were the ground floor
Delicate slender fingers define the feminine
Energy fluxed across corporeal bounds

We came to experience – food, ourselves
Establish a spiritual resonance
An Asian table d'hote was the catalyst
Part audience, part maestro, it was music

Behind yellow parchment lay a story
For weeks, I imagined you – aching to know
And for me, the key to someone's soul

<Tell me about the book>

Your humanity filled the room,
stilling the air
Edgy gave way to gentle depth
Depth invited trust and courage
In a moment I became special

A book tells a story.
Wanting it, reveals a person.

Like a slow clock, each dish marked our time

Tastes, sips, smiles, laughs, words, and again

<Her voice is many colored silk>

Faces swapped expressions
Like card players we learned the deck

Time s-t-r-e-t-c-h-e-d,
pulled by wine and tales
Until the horizon slowly revealed
Future, past, seconds, days, years
The currents of history reach a confluence

Your body met mine as our metronome **stopped**
Time came to a single point
Meld, form and fuse
Emotions interwoven as desire and heat

My hands _searched_ the passion of your form
Luxurious skin speaks to my touch
I _roamed_ the hidden down as my hold gripped
And then ever so quietly, t-i-c-k t-o-c-k

Another occasion will come renewal

And stop the world

Perfect

Your warm presence invited.
  My gaze rested on the smooth
    bronze surface of your neck.
      One kiss. Two kisses.
        The electric tingle of my
          attention travelled through
            your body.
              Wanting more.
            Your head tilts back in an
          act of seduction.
        Entranced as if I were a mystic,
      you offered.
    My lips found their way with
the smallest of nibbles.

With your body heat rising
  with each marriage of my mouth
    and your skin,
      you gave more.
        Slowly the revealing of
          the swell of your breast.
            Wrapped in violet and begging
              my attention.
            Never has such a beautiful
          and sensual gift been shared.
        Nothing less than perfection.
      Flawless in its presentation and
    for the heart that lay below.
How could I be the one?

Moonbeams

The late hour beckons rest.

A fall moon casts its white shadow over your
nude figure.

I watch from across the room,
treated to nature's art.

Your gentle arms, raised to tie your long,
sweeping, dark tresses,
form a heart in the evening light.

Are you sending me a message of love?

My eyes leisurely trace the silhouette
presented by the darkness in the room and the
affection of the evening.

Your rounded face, leads to a smooth neckline,
a trek for my gaze.

Down your shoulders,
to the rise of your breast,
peaked by the raised nipple,
to form a consummate image of woman.

My admiring stare slides down
your divine belly,
to the roundness of broad hips,
finally falling to teasing legs.

Slowly turning your head,
you catch my look,
knowing, not imagining,
what possesses my thoughts.

A warm smile appears on your face,
with a shine in your eyes as you respond to
me with nothing more than a look.

Discovered in the act,
I move to you,
my body next to yours,
and I feel the
sensation of your skin against my mine.

My hands begin the journey
over your body
following the footsteps
just made by my eyes.

Your hands reach behind and
touch my hair,
you turn to feel my beard
against your cheek.

My hands wrapped your waist,
I feel the gentle delicacy of
your lips as you
kiss my face.

In a musical whisper you
guide the moment,
"Bed time".

From its place in the heavens,
the moon watches.

Sunrise Ocean

Morning and evening
  the golden rays of the star
    lord over the broad oceans

From one view,
  you stand in gaze;
    it is dawn

The vast landscape
  of waves hide from light

Beneath,
  an aqua life breathes in the flows,
    uninterested in the wonders
      about to unfold

The sharp line
  between sea and sky becomes sharpened,
    drawn by an artist's pencil

      Sol is an ancient spirit,
        asleep for hours

      Heavy lidded,
    conscienceness arrives
      at a ponderous pace

      The lashes lift
     in a display of arcs
   that skirt across whitecaps

     You close your eyes,
    spreading out your arms,
   you sense the beams of morning
     touch your skin,
    as if you're a leaf

  The echo of the surf fills your senses,
   the salt chases your nose,
    as you strain to feel
     the coming heat

You look again at the eastern horizon.
Half-awake the giant presence
regards you on the beach

In a world with only you in witness,
you shed your garments
to feel the rise of
nature without a barrier

The emerging reds and yellows
cast their glance over your skin,
across you face, shoulders, breasts,
in journey to your toes

Arms outstretched you wait for more
breadth of the dawn

The music of the water and
the paintbrush of the sun
create the masterpiece you seek

From a distance
I see you in this painting

It is beauty, defined
Until dusk

At Rest

Calm has swept over your body

Passion sated, you drift away
Your back, hips shine in faint moonlight

Face, eyes hidden in slumber,
your dark locks frame

you   like
a   picture

As air fills your chest,
I watch your back rise and
f
  a
    l
     l

I am hypnotized by you,
our experience, my emotions,
and the rhythm of your form

My hand **t r a c e s** the movement,
d
  o
    w
      n your back, over graceful mounds,
to smooth legs

You breathe but do not stir
I watch and do not sleep
Who can, with such vision at hand

Yet we both rest, for now

Photograph

It's the slight curl of your lip
melted into a pout
you rarely share.

It's the peak-a-boo show with
your dark devil's eyes and
the perfect shading
of hypnotic locks.

It's the fall look,
part obscured,
yet revealed
limbs speaking of the muscled,
feminine mystique below.

Yet the photo speaks to a man.
To me.

Maybe I'll take you in my mouth
with these teasing lips.
You know what I do.
The torture I give.
The pleasure that follows.

Maybe I want to feel your animal pace.
My legs mounting your shoulders
as you define the male beast.

Maybe I want to drive my pleasure,
your wrists pinned under my strength,
my hips riding you like my steed,
taking what I want in my moment of greed.

Maybe I want it all.
Because that's the life I'm living.

Devotion

My devotion is not my own.

You dance with me to express its beauty.

Giving is easy, but valued only when received

I want him to give, it's a love for me.

A love I want to treasure.

**What shall I ask so that he knows
        I love him?**

You receive my worship. I receive your need.

I need you to care for me.
        Tell me what to do.

Who is the dominant? Who serves?

Am I giving because
        I await your request for leadership?

**He wants my success.
        My good. My happiness.**

Doesn't every lover want that?

Is it really devotion if
        it just feels like love.

On your knees. Give.

I want. I can't refuse him.

My soul wants to be needed.

His want is need. For me.

Who is devoted?

You approach with your cherry red lips
        A closeup in Film Noir

Bright ivory gleams with fiendish thoughts
        Scented breath as you lean in

A bite.
        Intimate. Demanding. Commanding.
And giving.

Who is devoted?

Wait until I summon you. No touching.

Pure obedience.

I have a ritual for you.

She creates transcendence. I'm lost.

But finding gems in my primal thoughts.

Who is devoted?

We ride a highway of emotion, unleashed

Both grabbing the wheel, a grinning dance

Navigation of passions.

Giving.
        Gifted.
                Reviving.
                        Received.

And devotion.

FORCED

She is contradiction.
Restraint with Demand.
Intimate yet distant.
Need and withdrawal.

One constant. Passion. Over and over.

One. Many. Unbound. Unlimited.

Organic urgency. Raw drive.

A moment begins, animal want.

Rough lips. Firm hands. Clothing askew.

Hold me. Bind me. Force me.

I do. Acting, or not?

Warm flesh, tight skin, erect need.
I take. You obey, our dance.

Fingers graze, we move in chorus.

Find me. Feel me. Force me.

Bodies lock, familiar and fresh.
I find your key. Your form goes limp.

My mouth devours. My fingers restrain.

Tighter. Hold me. Push me. Force me.

I want. I need. I reveal.
Taut and full.
Blood Crimson with violent demand.

Take me. Now. Enter now. Force me.

Hearts screaming. Eyes watching.
Dominant thrust. Pressure on dampness.

Push. Force me.

I drink you, fully joined.
Stretch. Moan. More.

Firm grasp. Filling heat. Passioned wince.

Again. Force me.

Weight. Piston strength, desperation.
Bold rhythms. Rising hunger.

Tight smile. Fired stare.

From depths, her cry.

Force me.

Again.

And again.

I do.

Gasping. Blind instinct. Cresting heights.

Force me.

I will.

Again. And again.

Relinquish

Trust is the **mother** of submission

Pleasure is it's **father**

As a **mother,**
she was unequalled
in my lifetime

As a **father,**
she defied all imagination

Discipline revealed through equal parts
intellect and Eros

Submission showed faith, desire

But the lessons,
gifted **teacher,**
thoughtful **parent**

Planned. Imagined. Executed ...

A curriculum of pain,
pleasure,
domination,
obedience

My soul compelled to
fuse animal desire and
erudite reasoning

Mystery and theater
craft an enduring memory

On my knees
Blinded

The rapt **pupil**,
offspring,
ceding honor, devotion

I serve her orgasm with privilege,
my mouth an instrument of sexual art

Exploring **deity** from my place of fealty

I taste all of sides of
your offered **divine feminine**

It's adoration even
if compelled to pleasure

Her hand taught
harsh lessons

Bestowed with love,
as only pain can be

I sought, she gave

Matching urges,
was a samba for
our erotic arts

The ultimate humility,
but not humiliation

Goddess in her fullness,
subject supine before her,
finally penetrated

My sight returned to a
vision of her

A **female strength**
I have not known

Celestial woman, part demon

Such energy had taken
possession of body

Wielding a purified
carnal pleasure
with mine

Intense, urgent,
needful, commanding.

Her burning pace,
intoxicating,
beyond sexual passion

Wanton raw heat

Finally love
Penetration of my body
Penetration of hers
My release

This journey I worshipped
at her altar of pleasure

I wanted to be owned

**By a Goddess,
an Angel,
an Erotic apparition**

And I was
        Unconditionally, Wholly
                Exclusively hers

ww.w.ingramcontent.com/pod-product-compliance
Lightning Source LLC
Chambersburg PA
CBHW052214090426
42741CB00010B/2539